For Mary Brigid Barrett, Richard, Elizabeth, Emily and
Patrick Groth, a song of praise and thanksgiving —K. P.

For Rebecca, Kristin, and Benjamin, my shining stars,
precious and fair, and for Saint Francis, who reminds
us to be ever grateful —P. D.

Text © 2011 by Minna Murra, Inc. • Illustrations © 2011 by Pamela Dalton • All rights reserved
No part of this book may be reproduced in any form without written permission from the
publisher • Library of Congress Cataloging-in-Publication Data available • ISBN 978-0-8118-
7734-3 • Book design by Amelia May Anderson • Typeset in Sonopa • The illustrations in this
book were rendered with cut paper and watercolor • Manufactured by Toppan Leefung, Da Ling
Shan Town, Dongguan, China, in Jan 2012 • 10 9 8 7 6 5 4 3 • This product conforms
to CPSIA 2008 • Handprint Books is an imprint of Chronicle Books LLC
680 Second Street, San Francisco, California 94107 • www.chroniclekids.com

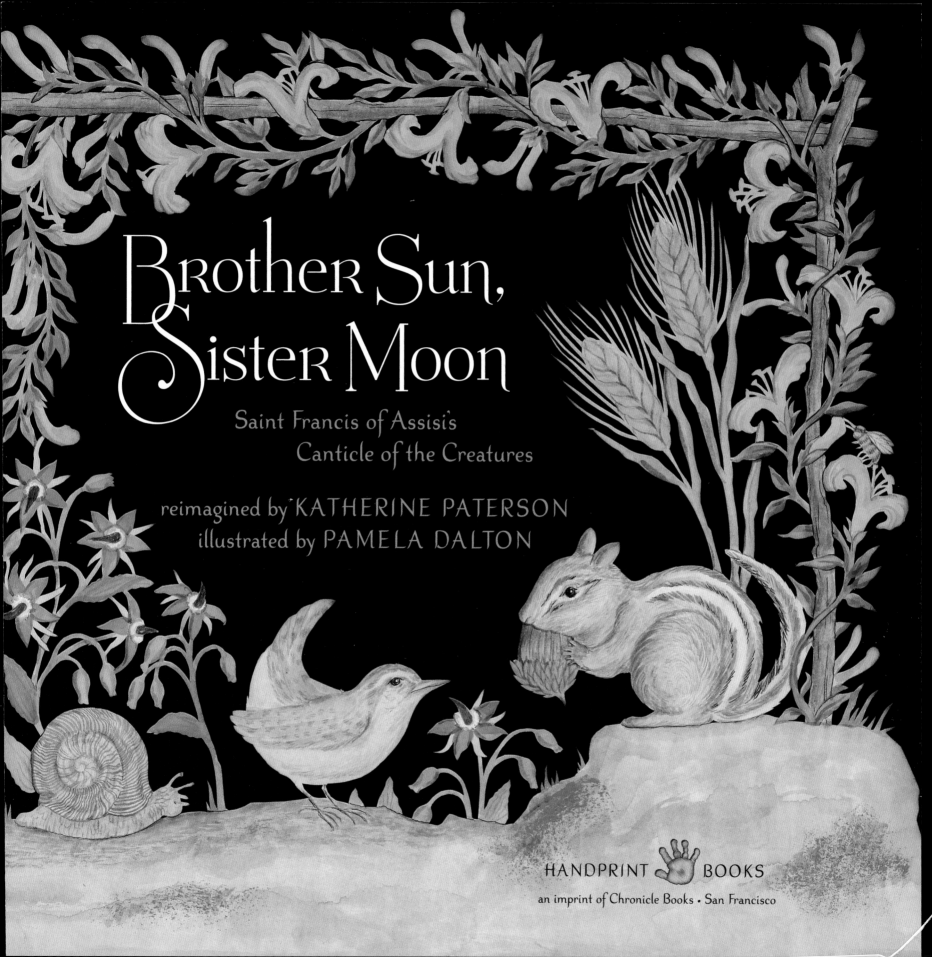

Brother Sun, Sister Moon

Saint Francis of Assisi's
Canticle of the Creatures

reimagined by KATHERINE PATERSON
illustrated by PAMELA DALTON

HANDPRINT BOOKS

an imprint of Chronicle Books · San Francisco

We come to sing a song of praise to you,
O God, the Lord of Heaven and Earth.

who by your power and out of your love have
created all things and called them good.

We praise you for our Brother Sun.
who in his radiant dawning

every day reminds us that it was
you who brought forth light.

We praise you for Sister Moon and all
our Sister Stars, who clothe the night

with their beauty and, like you,
watch over us while we sleep.

We praise you for our Brother Wind and every kind of weather, stormy or mild. For when he roars he reminds us of your might, and when he comes as a cooling breeze, he tells us of your gentleness.

Praise, too, for our ever-present Brother Air, who, though invisible, surrounds us and gives us life and breath.

Truly, he is a creation in your likeness.

We praise you for Sister Water, who fills the seas and
rushes down the rivers—who wells up from the earth

and falls down from heaven—who gives herself
that all living things may grow and be nourished.

We praise you for our Brother Fire, whose strength warms our homes

and in whose
resplendent dancing
light we glimpse
your playfulness.

We praise you for
our Sister Earth, who declares
your mother love for us

as she sustains our
bodies with food and our
souls with beauty.

We praise you
for the ones
among us who
forgive those
who have
wronged them
in the same spirit
as you constantly
forgive us.

And for those who must bear in this life sickness and trial, we ask for the comfort of your everlasting arms.

We praise you that in this world of hatred and war,
you still give us courageous brothers and sisters

who offer their lives to the making of peace.
They are indeed your beloved children.

And, though we often fear her, we praise you for our Sister Death, who will usher us at last into

your loving presence, where we will know and
love you as you have always known and loved us.

For all your gifts—for this wondrous universe in which we live, for family, for friends, for work and play,

for this life and the life to come—
we sing our praise to you.

For this life and
the life to come, we
sing our praise to you,
O Lord, the Father
and Mother of all
creation.
Give us, we pray,
the grace to honor you
this day and
forever more.

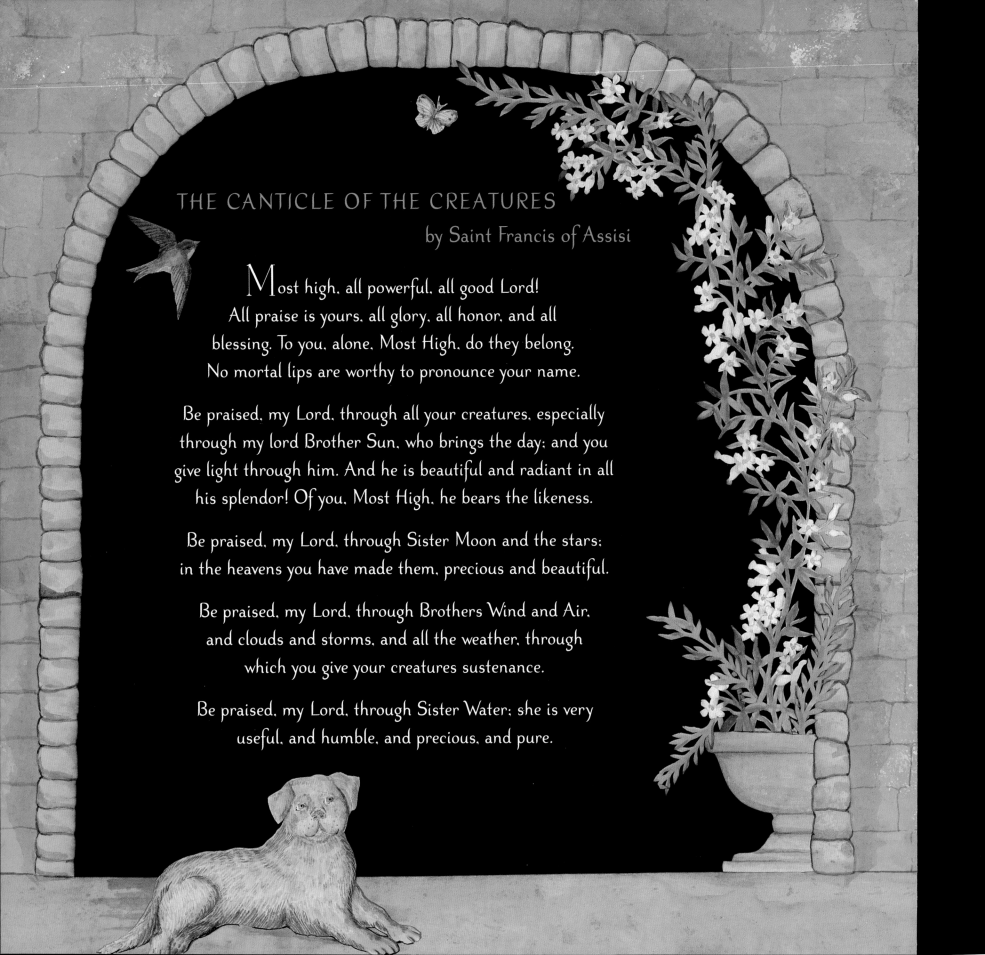

THE CANTICLE OF THE CREATURES
by Saint Francis of Assisi

Most high, all powerful, all good Lord!
All praise is yours, all glory, all honor, and all
blessing. To you, alone, Most High, do they belong.
No mortal lips are worthy to pronounce your name.

Be praised, my Lord, through all your creatures, especially
through my lord Brother Sun, who brings the day; and you
give light through him. And he is beautiful and radiant in all
his splendor! Of you, Most High, he bears the likeness.

Be praised, my Lord, through Sister Moon and the stars;
in the heavens you have made them, precious and beautiful.

Be praised, my Lord, through Brothers Wind and Air,
and clouds and storms, and all the weather, through
which you give your creatures sustenance.

Be praised, my Lord, through Sister Water; she is very
useful, and humble, and precious, and pure.

Be praised. my Lord. through Brother Fire.
through whom you brighten the night. He is beautiful
and cheerful and powerful and strong.

Be praised. my Lord. through our Sister Mother Earth.
who feeds us and rules us and produces various
fruits with colored flowers and herbs.

Be praised. my Lord. through those who forgive
for love of you: through those who endure sickness
and trial. Happy those who endure in peace. for
by you. Most High. they will be crowned.

Be praised. my Lord. through our
Sister Bodily Death. from whose embrace
no living person can escape. Woe to
those who die in mortal sin! Happy those
she finds doing your most holy will. The second
death can do no harm to them.

Praise and bless my Lord. and give thanks.
and serve him with great humility.

Translated by Bill Barrett from the Umbrian text of the *Assisi codex*.
Used with permission.
www.webster.edu/~barrettb/canticle.htm

How do you "reimagine" the words of the most beloved saint in the history of Christendom? If I hadn't been so taken with the samples I saw of Pamela Dalton's art, I don't think I'd have tried. But as I began rereading the text of *The Canticle of the Sun*, with this book in mind, I found my heart, in John Wesley's words, "strangely warmed." It was such a wonderful exercise to see myself as close kin to all the rest of the natural world—sun, moon, stars, wind, and weather—even to look death in the face and call her my sister. In the effort to make this Canticle my own song of praise, I understood what Francis meant when, in another of his poems, he declares, "I have come to learn God adores His creation."*

—Katherine Paterson

*From "God Would Kneel Down," by Saint Francis of Assisi, included in *Love Poems from God*, collected by Daniel Ladinsky. Penguin, 1999.

Editor's note: It is written that Saint Francis of Assisi (1181–1226) composed the *Laudes Creaturarum* ("Praise Song of the Creatures"—or as it has often become known, *The Canticle of the Sun*) in the final two years of his life, at a time when he was already almost completely blind, in the village of San Damiano, while under the care of Saint Clare and the sisters of her monastery. Francis chose to write in his local Umbrian dialect, rather than the Latin spoken in the church, so that his words could be understood by all.

Many years ago I saw my first papercuttings. They were such an exciting mystery. How did people do this? I decided to find out. I experimented for a long time, trying different cutting tools, different kinds of paper, and different cutting surfaces. Eventually, I found the combination that worked comfortably for me. The patterns I started with were very simple ones. I tried cutting the paper with one fold, two folds, and three folds, and sometimes no folds at all. Many pieces wound up in the trash can, but I did not give up. Over time, I developed a careful technique, cutting each picture out of a single piece of paper. Then, using a method popular in early nineteenth-century Pennsylvania German communities, I painted the papercuts with watercolors.

I started going to Italy several years ago to study painting; many times I stayed in Assisi where Saint Francis was born and lived. I came to know about his life and his work: He took on the life of a poor man, not even owning a pair of shoes. He dedicated himself to God by taking care of the sick, the hungry, and the needy. Francis loved all people wherever he went. But he also loved the animals, birds, and all the elements of Nature.

Saint Francis's prayer, *The Canticle of the Creatures*, reminds us to love, to revere, and to take care of this beautiful world in which we live and all the beings who dwell within it.

—Pamela Dalton